FAITH

Five Religions and What They Share

Written and photographed by

Dr. Richard Steckel and Michele Steckel

Kids Can Press

To good-hearted people everywhere whose lives are filled with
passionate kindness, acceptance, respect for others and gratitude.
— Richard and Michele Steckel

A note on dates

B.C.E. stands for "before the common era" or "before the current era." It means the same thing as B.C.,
which stands for "before Christ." B.C.E. is used out of respect for the many people in the world who do
not follow Christianity.

Text by Robin Simons and Jenny Lehman
Text and photographs © 2012 Milestones Project

Kids Can Press acknowledges the financial support of the Government of Ontario, through the
Ontario Media Development Corporation's Ontario Book Initiative; the Ontario Arts Council;
the Canada Council for the Arts; and the Government of Canada, through the BPIDP, for our
publishing activity.

Published in Canada by
Kids Can Press Ltd.
25 Dockside Drive
Toronto, ON M5A 0B5

Published in the U.S. by
Kids Can Press Ltd.
2250 Military Road
Tonawanda, NY 14150

www.kidscanpress.com

Edited by Valerie Wyatt
Designed by Julia Naimska

This book is smyth sewn casebound.
Manufactured in Singapore, in 10/2011 by Tien Wah Press (Pte) Ltd.

CM 12 0 9 8 7 6 5 4 3 2 1

Library and Archives Canada Cataloguing in Publication

Steckel, Richard
     Faith : five religions and what they share / Richard Steckel and Michele Steckel.

Includes index.
For ages 8–12.
ISBN 978-1-55453-750-1

1. Religions—Juvenile literature. I. Steckel, Michele II. Title.

BL92.S84 2012   j200   C2011-904725-X

Kids Can Press is a *l'orus*™ Entertainment company

Contents

What is faith?

Faith is what is in our hearts and minds.

Faith is when you trust something you cannot see or touch, but you believe it exists.

Faith helps us feel peaceful and secure.

Where do we come from? Where do we go when we die? Why are we here? How should we live? Why do bad things happen?

For as long as people have walked the earth, they have pondered these questions. Faith helps provide answers.

There are twenty-two major religions in the world plus many, many smaller ones, and there are many differences between them. But at the heart of every religion is faith: the belief that there is something larger than us, larger than our universe. Faith is something beyond what we can see, hear and touch that gives meaning to our lives.

This book explores five of the world's most widely practiced religions: Buddhism, Christianity, Hinduism, Islam and Judaism. Although each of these religions began in one part of the world, all have now spread and are practiced by millions of people on many continents.

Each of these religions has its own special stories, beliefs, objects and rituals. But they also have many things in common and share many elements of faith. The following pages will show you the different ways that religions help people celebrate and make sense of the world and also the many aspects of faith that religions share.

Christianity

Understanding religions

Long ago, faith bound people together. Praying together for sun and rain, for a bountiful crop or for a good hunt helped people feel that they had greater control over an unpredictable world. Over time, new ideas about faith and new religions developed, and as they did, tensions arose. Some people felt threatened by the new, and those who held the new beliefs felt that the old ways were wrong. Violence broke out among people of different religions, and throughout history, misunderstandings between religions have led to frequent conflicts.

Unfortunately, religious conflicts continue today. Across the globe — in the Middle East, Africa, Asia and Europe — fighting continues between Christians, Jews, Muslims and Hindus, between Protestants and Catholics and between followers of other religions.

Islam

Conflict sometimes happens in our own communities, too. Instead of seeing those of other faiths as people like us, we first see their differences. We see a girl in a headscarf and think "Muslim" instead of seeing that she is a young woman with concerns and feelings like our own. We see a boy in a small black skullcap and think "Jew" before we notice the T-shirt and sneakers that are similar to our own.

Perhaps if we recognized that all faiths are more alike than they are different, we could replace intolerance with respect. Perhaps if we learned more about one another's religions, we would have fewer reasons for misunderstandings, conflicts or even wars.

Faith helps people feel God
within themselves – regardless
of what religion they are.

Working together for peace

Even in the parts of the world that are torn by religious conflict, there are people of different faiths working together to create peace. How can you help make peace in your own community?
Take a LEAP of faith.

Learn about other religions.

Educate others.

Appreciate the differences.

Play with kids of other religions — nothing creates bonds better than play.

Judaism

Five major religions

These major religions — Buddhism, Christianity, Hinduism, Islam and Judaism — have evolved over thousands of years. Perhaps it is human nature, but when we compare things, we often first see what makes one thing different from another. As you read about these religions, look for their differences and their similarities. You may be surprised by how much they have in common.

Hinduism

Judaism

Christianity

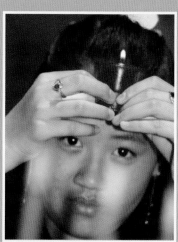
Buddhism

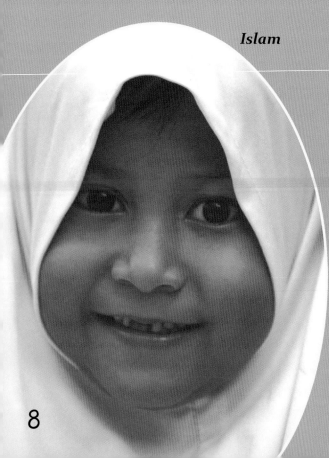
Islam

How Many Followers? Where Are They?

There is no official count of how many people practice each religion, and every religion has followers all over the world. But the chart below will give you an idea of how many people follow each religion and where they live.

RELIGION	NUMBER	WHERE MOST FOLLOWERS LIVE
Buddhism	376 million	Asia
Christianity	2.1 billion	Worldwide
Hinduism	900 million	India
Islam	1.6 billion	Middle East, Africa, Asia
Judaism	14 million	North America, Israel, Europe

Buddhism

B uddhism began in India about 2500 years ago (approximately 500 B.C.E.). At that time, most of the people of India believed that they were caught in a continuous cycle of life, death and rebirth called reincarnation. For most people, life was filled with difficulty, suffering and unfairness, so they were eager to find an escape from this cycle.

In about 500 B.C.E., a man named Siddhartha Gautama thought and meditated until he understood how to escape the cycle and reach *nirvana*, a state of peace and detachment from the world. He came to be called the Buddha, which means "the enlightened one." His teachings are the basis of Buddhism.

The Buddha taught people to free themselves from attachment to the things of this world and from pain and suffering. Many Buddhists take the *bodhisattva* vow, which means dedicating their lives to the service of others.

Buddhism

Christianity

Christianity began 2000 years ago with the teachings of Jesus. Jesus was born a Jew in what is now the Palestinian Territories. His followers believed him to be the Messiah, the savior whom God had promised to send to the Jewish people. Jesus preached that people should love one another as God loved them.

His popularity made Jesus a threat to politicians, and they had him crucified (nailed up on a cross). The Christian scriptures say that, days after his crucifixion, Jesus was resurrected (rose from the dead). He met with his disciples before going up to heaven to be with God. Christians believe that Jesus's death and resurrection help them to forgive and be forgiven, and that it offers the promise of eternal life.

Christianity spread and became the world's largest religion. As it grew, it split into different branches. The largest branches are the Roman Catholic, Eastern Orthodox and Protestant churches.

Hinduism

Hinduism

The traditions that are now called Hinduism began more than 3500 years ago (between 2000 and 1500 B.C.E.) in what is now India. The majority of Indian people are still Hindu. There are many different ways to practice Hinduism but central to all of them is Brahman. Brahman is the spirit, or power, beyond our universe and understanding — what many people call God.

Hindus also worship thousands of lesser gods and goddesses whose stories are told in Hinduism's sacred texts. The result is an enormous variety of religious traditions, ranging from small groups to major religious movements with millions of followers. Hinduism grants complete freedom of belief and worship — there is no "wrong" religion or way of faith.

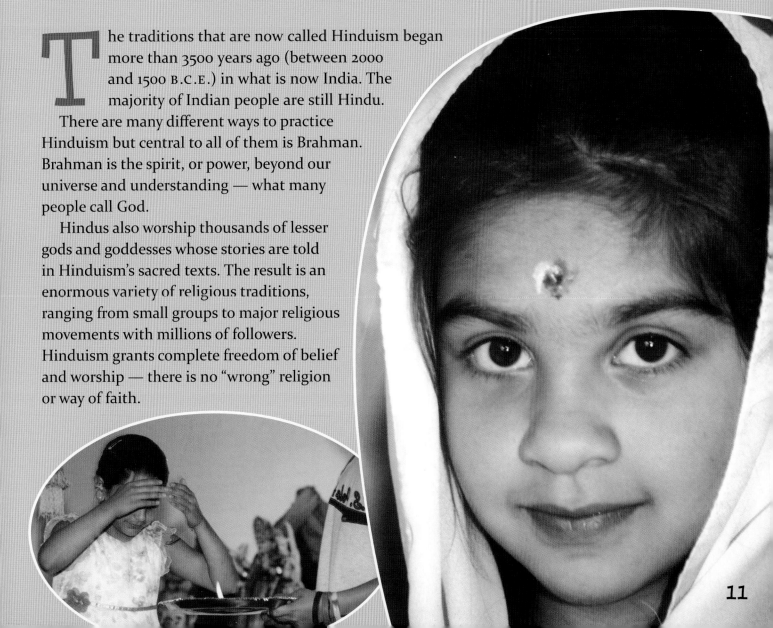

Islam

Islam began more than 1400 years ago (in the year 610) when Muhammad ibn Abdullah was meditating on a mountain near Mecca in what is now Saudi Arabia. As he meditated, he received the word of God. Since that time, Muhammad has been considered the prophet of Islam. "Islam" means "submission to God." Followers of Islam are called Muslims.

Unlike most of the people in Arabia who believed in many gods, Muhammad believed that there was only one God — Allah. The Qur'an, the Muslim holy book, was revealed to him verse by verse over the next twenty-one years, often in response to a crisis or a question.

Muslims maintain that the Qur'an is the word of God. They are expected to follow Islamic law (shar'iah), which touches on almost every aspect of life and society — Islam is a complete way of life. The Qur'an presents the "five pillars of Islam," a framework for worship and signs of commitment to the faith.

They are: believing there is only one god and that Muhammad is his messenger; praying five times a day; fasting during the holy month of Ramadan; giving to the poor; and making a pilgrimage to Mecca at least once in a lifetime.

Islam

Islam

Judaism

Judaism

Judaism began about 4000 years ago among the Hebrew (or Israelite) people in the Middle East. According to the Hebrew Bible, God promised a man named Abraham that he would take care of Abraham's people forever, if they would obey his laws. This agreement, or covenant, is the basis of Judaism. Later, God spoke to Moses and gave him commandments, including the Ten Commandments, which are laws and guiding principles for how to live as a Jew.

For Jewish people, Judaism is not only their religion, it's their way of life. The main branches of Judaism are Orthodox, Conservative, Reform and Reconstructionist, and each has different principles that guide the way their followers live and worship. But all promote a belief in one God and uphold Jewish law, which sets out how a person should behave toward others.

Three Religions, One Ancestor

Abraham is considered the father, or patriarch, not just of Judaism, but also of Islam and Christianity. All three religions revere Abraham, who brought to the world the concept of one God. In fact, Christianity, Islam and Judaism are sometimes called Abrahamic faiths, after Abraham.

Judaism

Many religions, one Golden Rule

The five religions instruct followers on how they should behave toward others. The words are different but the thoughts are surprisingly similar.

"Whatever you wish that others would do to you, do so to them." — Christianity

"One should not behave toward others in a way which is disagreeable to oneself." — Hinduism

"Comparing oneself to others in such terms as 'Just as I am so are they, just as they are so am I,' he should neither kill nor cause others to kill." — Buddhism

"Not one of you is a believer until he loves for his brother what he loves for himself." — Islam

"You shall love your neighbor as yourself." — Judaism

Your Golden Rule

All the quotes above from the major world religions say the same thing: Treat others as you would have them treat you. This is often called the Golden Rule. Work with your family or classmates to come up with your own Golden Rule. Put your Golden Rule on a wall or on the refrigerator to remind you of your shared values.

Spiritual leaders

In every religion, spiritual leaders help worshippers practice their faith.

In the Jewish faith, the *rabbi* leads prayers, teaches about Judaism and offers help and advice to people in need. However, Jewish congregations do not require a rabbi, and some worship without one. In most branches of Judaism, rabbis can be men or women.

Although Hindus worship mostly at home, they also visit temples. There, a priest acts as an intermediary between the people and the gods. He makes offerings to the gods on behalf of the worshippers and invites the gods to join them.

In a Christian church, the religious leader may be called a priest, minister, pastor, reverend or father. Traditionally, Christian religious leaders were men, but today, approximately one-eighth are women. In the Eastern Orthodox and Roman Catholic branches of Christianity, the leaders are still always men.

Buddhism

Christianity

In Islam, the *imam* is the religious leader. He (imams are always male) leads prayers, teaches about Islam and offers guidance to the members of his congregation.

Several religions have monks and nuns. Monks (men) and nuns (women) devote themselves to prayer or meditation. They often live in monasteries and wear simple clothes. They do not marry and avoid the use of money. These behaviors set them apart from the world and help them devote themselves to their religious practice.

Buddhist monks and nuns serve as teachers of the *dharma* (Buddha's teachings). Although some Buddhists choose to become monks for their whole lives, others may live as monks in a monastery for only a short time in order to learn and meditate.

Sacred texts

The five major religions have sacred texts, or books, that contain God's teachings and messages. Some people believe that the texts contain God's actual words, and that they must be followed precisely. Others believe that the texts were written by people to record God's words and intentions, and that the texts can be understood in different ways. In all religions that came into being before the written word, the stories in the texts were passed down orally for generations before they were finally written down.

In Judaism, the most sacred text is called the Torah. It contains the commandments and stories that God gave to Moses. Some people believe that the words of the Torah are literally God's words. Others believe that Moses wrote down what he understood God to say. Still others believe that many scholars wrote the Torah.

Each Torah is hand-lettered in Hebrew on a scroll made of parchment. Because it is a sacred object made of fragile material, Jews do not touch the Torah with their hands. Instead, they use a pointer called a *yad*, which means "hand" in Hebrew. Two ornate caps called rimmonim decorate the tops of the Torah. The *rimmonim* usually contain bells, which ring as the Torah is carried around the synagogue.

Christianity

The Christian Bible is made up of two books: the Old and New Testaments. The Old Testament is almost exactly the same as the Jewish Torah (although the Torah contains other Jewish texts). The New Testament is the story and teachings of Jesus and the early Christian church.

Judaism

Islam

The sacred text of Islam is the Qur'an. It contains the words that Allah spoke to Muhammad. The Qur'an is always written in Arabic, the language of Muhammad, which is still spoken throughout the Middle East.

Hinduism has more sacred texts than any other major religion. These are called the Vedas, the Upanishads, the Bhagavad Gita, the Ramayana and the Mahabharata. They are written in Sanskrit, the ancient language of India, and contain teachings, hymns and stories about the thousands of Hindu gods and goddesses.

Buddhism also has many texts that convey the teachings of the Buddha, including the *sutras* and the *suttas*. One important collection of Buddha's teachings is called the Tipitaka, which means "three baskets," because it was originally written on palm leaves that were collected together in baskets.

Hinduism

Learning about other people's religions helps us see that we are all more alike than we are different, and that we are all children of a single great spirit.

 Rules to live by

Most religious books contain stories and rules to live by. Write five rules you think are important. Then use a variety of beautiful papers, stickers and decorations to make an ornate book. Write your rules to live by in it. Write stories to illustrate each rule.

Clothing

Wearing special clothes (or even just "good clothes") is one way people show respect for God. For example, in many religions, people cover their heads to show that they are humble in God's presence.

When they pray, Jewish boys (and some girls) wear skullcaps called *kippahs* or *yarmulkes*. Some also wear a shawl called a *tallit*. The tallit makes them feel as if they are wrapped in God's love. The fringes of the tallit remind Jews to obey God's commandments. Orthodox Jewish women always keep their heads covered. In the last hundred years, one way to obey the faith but stay fashionable has been to wear a wig instead of a scarf.

Muslims believe that men and women should dress modestly so as not to attract the attention of the opposite sex. Muslim women and girls must cover their heads to pray. Men and boys do not have to cover their heads, but many choose to wear a skullcap called a *kufi*. All Muslims remove their shoes when they pray.

The headscarf worn by Muslim girls is called a *hijab*, which means "covering." Some Muslim women wear headscarves in public, others wear veils that

Judaism

Islam

hide their faces, and some leave their heads uncovered.

The various branches of Hinduism have other traditions about religious clothing. For example, widows are supposed to dress in white. While most Hindu women wear a headscarf at all times, some wear it only to pray.

Christianity has the fewest traditions about religious clothing, except for priests and nuns. Even they have a rather wide range of garments, depending on their traditions. Some nuns are covered from head to toe with a "habit," while other nuns just wear ordinary clothing. Most Christians generally follow one rule: Be respectful in your choice of clothing. However, in an effort to draw more young people into this faith, many modern churches welcome people who wear very casual clothes.

The one exception for Christians is wearing white for special ceremonies. When babies or older people are baptized as Christians, they wear white clothes. Also, when a Catholic child receives his or her first communion (see page 22), the child often wears white. A girl's first communion is considered especially important, and families will buy or make the most beautiful white dress they can afford.

Often the most distinctive clothes are reserved for spiritual teachers and leaders.

The clothes may be plain or ornate to symbolize the important connection between a teacher and God.

A Buddhist monk wears a simple yellow, orange or brown robe, similar to robes worn at the time of the Buddha. The simplicity of the robe is a reminder that being attached to material things causes suffering rather than happiness.

Jewish rabbis do not wear special robes or uniforms. They dress just like everybody else, even during services. Most, however, wear a yarmulke every day. Orthodox rabbis and other Jewish men always wear a black suit with a

white shirt, a tallit and a black hat. They also have beards. All of these clothing traditions remind people to worship God.

Christian religious leaders usually wear robes over their street clothes. The robes may be simple or ornate, depending on the church. Some Christian religious leaders also wear special hats. For example, Catholic religious leaders wear a skullcap called a *zucchetto* during services, while Greek Orthodox priests often wear long black robes and a black "chimney pot" hat.

Christianity

Symbols

In every faith, people use special objects to remind them of God's love and teachings and to help them pray.

The main symbol of Judaism is a six-pointed star. It is called the Star of David after King David who, 3000 years ago, ruled Israel, where the Jews lived. The *menorah*, a candlestick with seven branches, is another ancient symbol of Judaism because a menorah was lit every morning in the very first temple in Jerusalem. On the holiday of Hanukkah, Jews light a special nine-branch menorah. On Rosh Hashanah, the Jewish New Year, Jews think about how they will lead better lives in the year to come. At prayer services, they blow a ram's horn called a *shofar*, which "wakes them up" so they can prepare for the new year and repent the mistakes they made during the old one.

Jews have symbols, but they believe strongly that there should be no images of God. In fact, many Jews believe you should not say or write the name of God — instead, some write G-d as a sign of respect. Muslims also do not believe in having images of Allah, or of the prophet Muhammad.

Judaism

Judaism

Buddhist temples often have one or more prayer wheels. The wheels contain prayers printed on paper or parchment. Spinning the wheel is a way of saying the prayer. Many Buddhists also have a prayer flag made up of simple fabric squares decorated with messages to the Buddha tied onto a line. Meditating on a prayer flag as it flaps in the wind is a way of communicating one's faith that prayers will be answered.

Buddhists often use statues of the Buddha as symbols of worship. The statues can be small or massive. They show the Buddha in different positions (such as lying down, or laughing), but the traditional statue shows a serene Buddha sitting with legs crossed.

Hindus also have statues of the thousands of gods and goddesses they worship. These remind worshippers of their faith. Hindus make offerings of flowers, fruit and handmade gifts to the image of the god or goddess to whom they are devoted.

Islam has very few symbols compared to other religions. A crescent moon and star have no religious meaning, but are often used as symbols of Islam. The color green has a special place in Islam. It is used in the decoration of mosques, the bindings of Qur'ans and in the flags of

Buddhism

various Muslim countries. Some say green was Muhammad's favorite color and that he wore a green cloak and turban. Others believe that it symbolizes nature and life and is therefore a manifestation of God. The Qur'an says that the inhabitants of paradise will wear green garments of fine silk.

Hinduism

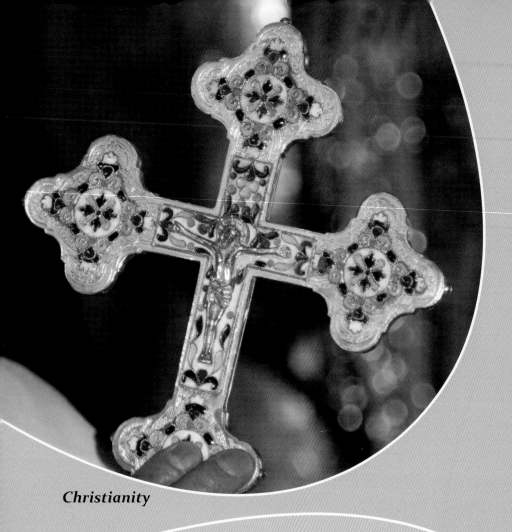

Christianity

Many Christians revere the symbol of a cross, which is a reminder that Jesus died on a cross and then rose from the dead to join God. His resurrection was seen as a sign of God's love for all people. A crucifix is similar to a cross, except that it includes the image of Jesus suffering on the cross.

Catholics have a rosary, a string of beads tied into a circle that includes a crucifix. They have a specific (although sometimes highly personalized) set of prayers or adorations for each bead on the rosary. You might hear someone comment that they are "saying the rosary." This means they are reciting a prayer as they hold each bead.

During the ceremony of Holy Communion, or the Eucharist, Christian worshippers sip a bit of wine and eat a small wafer or piece of bread. These remind people that Jesus gave his blood (symbolized by the wine) and his body (the bread) by dying on the cross. They are also a reminder of his promise to be with them for all time.

Shared Symbols

Islam

Many faiths use prayer beads to help worshippers count or concentrate on their prayers. You have read that Catholic prayer beads are called the rosary. Eastern Orthodox Christians use a prayer rope. Buddhist and Hindu prayer beads are called *malas*. Muslim *prayer* beads are called *tasbih* or *misbaha*.

In several faiths, a container called an ark or tabernacle holds sacred objects. In Jewish synagogues, the Torah is stored in an ark at the front of the room. In Catholic and Greek Orthodox churches, an ornate tabernacle holds the bread and wine that are used for Holy Communion.

Places of worship

All religions have large places of worship, such as temples or churches, in which people gather to pray. Some religions also emphasize worshipping at home. Whether in a public building or at home, prayers often are said facing a shrine or altar, which holds objects sacred to the faith.

Throughout India, there are very large Hindu temples elaborately decorated and dedicated to various gods or goddesses. Monks tend these places, which need upkeep because worshippers leave gifts of food that can spoil in the heat. Hindus worship at home more often than in temples. On their home altar, they place images of one or more gods or goddesses, as well as offerings, such as food, flowers and incense.

Christians worship primarily in churches, where the main service is held on Sunday. Churches may be ornate or simple but almost always have a prominent cross and a pulpit where the priest or minister stands to give a sermon.

Churches have long benches called "pews" for the worshippers to sit on and an altar where the bread and wine are kept. Many churches are built facing east toward Jerusalem because of its importance in the Bible and in the life of Jesus.

Christianity

Hinduism

The Jewish house of worship is called a synagogue. Every synagogue has an ark containing a Torah and an eternal light called a *ner tamid*, which represents the presence of God. Jews attend religious services on their Sabbath — sundown Friday to sundown Saturday. Synagogues are often built facing Jerusalem, the site of the first Jewish temple.

For Buddhists, meditation is a form of prayer. A Buddhist altar creates a space that invites people to sit and meditate. In addition to statues of Buddha and other teachers, it has candles, incense and flowers. Buddhists often have altars at home, as well as in their temples.

Buddhism

Islam

Muslims are expected to pray five times a day. When possible, they go to a *mosque*, where prayers are read from the Qur'an by the imam. Mosques have separate sections for men and women. When they cannot go to the mosque, Muslims pray at home or in any clean place, usually on a small prayer rug, which they carry with them.

A mosque can be very simple, such as a converted house or even an outdoor space. Or a mosque can be one of the largest and most elaborate buildings in a city, such as the Blue Mosque in Istanbul, Turkey (below). Formal mosques have a minaret, a tall tower where the imam climbs to call the faithful to prayer. Making adjustments for the modern world, many imams now use a loudspeaker mounted atop the minaret instead of climbing up themselves.

 # Visit a house of worship

Visit a house of worship or attend a service of a religion other than your own. Find five things that are the same as in your religion. Find five things that are different. What surprised you about the building or the service? If you could borrow something from that religion for your own, what would it be?

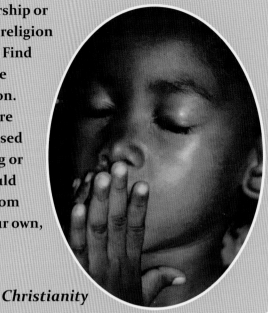

Christianity

Islam

Common acts of worship

While there are different forms of worship, many of the ways of expressing faith and devotion are common to all the major religions of the world.

Incense

Many faiths use incense in their ceremonies. The sweet smell of incense fills the space around the worshippers, symbolizing how God's presence fills the world. Many religions believe that the smoke rising from incense takes the worshippers' prayers toward heaven.

Sweet-smelling incense is lit as an offering on a Buddhist altar. Incense is also placed on a Hindu altar.

Formulas for making incense and directions for its use are found in the Jewish Torah and the Christian Bible. Jewish use of incense has fallen out of practice today, but incense is still used as part of many Christian services. For example, Greek Orthodox priests swing incense in a golden censor during prayer services in order to spread holiness around the church.

Buddhism

Christianity

26

Hinduism

Candles

Almost every religion uses candles in its ceremonies. The flickering light of candle flame is thought to embody God's presence.

At the beginning of the Jewish Sabbath, Jews light candles and say a blessing. The candles welcome peace, rest and God's presence into the house.

Both Judaism and Hinduism have a "festival of lights" every year, in which candles are prominent.

The Jewish festival is Hanukkah, which celebrates a miracle in the holy temple at Jerusalem long ago. The temple had been taken from the Jews. When it was returned to them, oil in a lamp that was only enough to last one day kept burning for eight days. The Jews felt their temple was restored to them, along with their ability to practice their religion. Jews have a special menorah called a *hanukiah* for this festival. It has nine candles. Eight candles represent the eight days. The ninth candle is used to light the others.

The Hindu festival of lights is Diwali, which celebrates different miraculous events for different sects. Still, for all Hindus, Diwali is a time for candles, oil lamps and firecrackers. It is a national holiday in India, and many Indian businesses choose to begin their financial year on the first day of Diwali.

Christianity

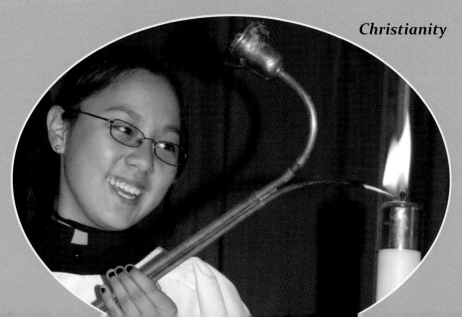

27

Actions during prayer

In many religions, special actions accompany prayer. Clasped hands, bowed heads and covered or closed eyes are common. They are all ways of showing respect for God.

Jewish women cover their eyes when they light the Sabbath candles. Jewish girls cover their eyes as they recite the holiest of Jewish prayers. Jewish parents commonly touch their children's heads and say a special prayer, asking God to grant the children health and happiness.

Hindus often cover their eyes when they pray, too. They bow in front of their altar to show gratitude to the gods. Boys and girls sometimes wear a dot of

Hinduism

powder, called a *tilak* or *bindi*, in the center of their foreheads. In different sects, this has different meanings. Sometimes it is used to show that a person is a Hindu. Sometimes it reminds people to see with "the third eye," or inner wisdom. Sometimes it is believed to protect people or to help them focus their goals for the day.

During prayers, many Christians kneel, bow their heads and clasp their hands to show their respect for God. Once a year, on Ash Wednesday, some Christians also wear a mark on their foreheads. The mark is made from ash and is applied in the shape of a cross. It

Christianity

Judaism

reminds people to repent their sins and to remember God. Ash Wednesday marks the beginning of the Christian season of Lent, the time of repentance, which ends with the celebration of Easter, the day marking Jesus's resurrection.

Buddhists bow to show gratitude for the teachings of the Buddha. They often sit cross-legged when they meditate. Hindus practice yoga, a form of body movement that helps them move toward a life of greater peace.

To show their submission to Allah, Muslims bow, kneel and lower their foreheads to the ground, then sit. They pray on prayer rugs and face the city of Mecca in Saudi Arabia, the most holy city in Islam.

Christianity

Islam

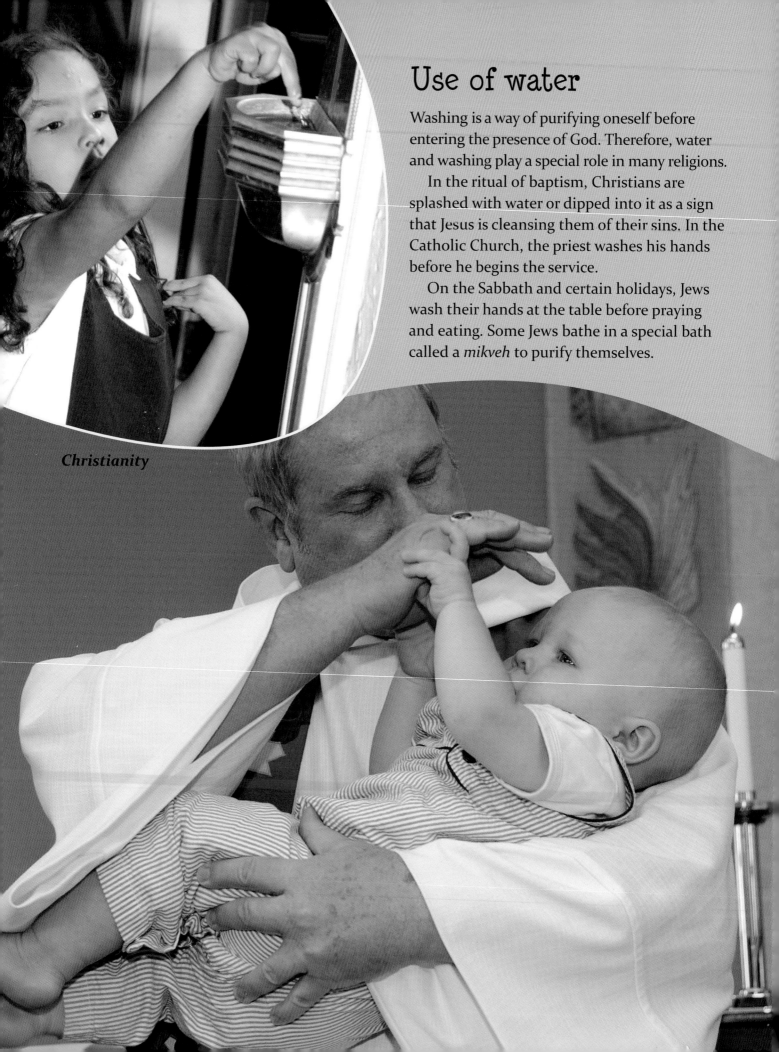

Use of water

Washing is a way of purifying oneself before entering the presence of God. Therefore, water and washing play a special role in many religions.

In the ritual of baptism, Christians are splashed with water or dipped into it as a sign that Jesus is cleansing them of their sins. In the Catholic Church, the priest washes his hands before he begins the service.

On the Sabbath and certain holidays, Jews wash their hands at the table before praying and eating. Some Jews bathe in a special bath called a *mikveh* to purify themselves.

Christianity

Muslims wash their faces, hands and feet before prayer and before touching the Qur'an to make sure they are pure in mind, body and heart.

Hindus wash before praying, preferably in running water. It is also considered a sacred obligation to take a holy bath before a festival. The most sacred water is that of the Ganges River (or *Ganga* in Sanskrit). Bathing in the river is believed to cause the remission of sins and helps free a person from the cycle of life and death. People travel long distances to immerse the ashes of their relatives in the waters of the Ganges, so that their loved ones will pass on to heaven.

In Buddhism, water is most often used as an offering. Water is one of the Four Elements (along with fire, air and earth). These natural elements lead to enlightenment, as opposed to the material world, which leads to suffering.

Islam

 # How do you pray?

Every religion has special prayers that are always said the same way. A prayer is a way of talking to a higher spirit. It can be a "thank you" for something good that happened or a request for help. It can be a quiet reflection or even a noisy outburst. Some people express prayers in words or poetry. Others use music, art or dance. Think of something in your life that has particular meaning for you and create your own prayer.

Buddhism

Charity

All of the five major religions consider it a sacred duty to help people who are less fortunate. Giving money, feeding the hungry, sheltering the homeless and comforting those in need are ways of bringing God's goodness into the world.

In Christianity, charity is considered the expression of God's love for people. By giving alms (money) and aid to the needy, Christians are spreading God's love.

In Buddhism, charity has three parts:
1. giving money and material goods to help the poor;
2. giving courage to those who are afraid; and
3. sharing the Buddha's teachings so that others can learn to live calmly and in peace.

Zakat (giving money to the poor) is one of the five pillars, or essential practices, of Islam. It is so important that it is considered a form of prayer.

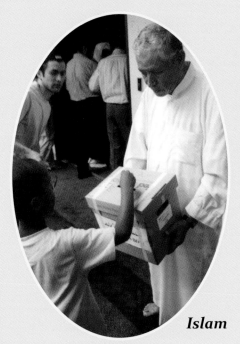

Islam

Performing *tsedaka* (helping the needy) is one of the most important laws in Judaism. Jewish tradition holds that beggars are sent by God to enable people with money to perform tsedaka. Jews put money in a tsedaka box at the synagogue for charity.

Hindus are required to give to the poor and help those in need. Like followers of other religions, they do so with no expectation of getting something in return.

Judaism

"No act of kindness, no matter how small, is ever wasted."

— Aesop

Cherishing children

Islam

Every religion encourages its followers to cherish their children because children are the future and the hope of every faith. In most religions, special rituals are used to welcome children into the faith and, often, to mark a child's passage into adulthood. Blessings for children are frequently said at religious services. Many sacred texts contain specific instructions to parents on how to honor and teach their children. All religions promote children's self-esteem because children who love and respect themselves are better able to love, respect and care for others.

In all five religions, it is considered important to teach children certain values. Respect for leaders and for the elderly are among those values, as are regular prayer, worship and charity.

All of the five religions expect parents to bring up their children in the ways of the faith. The religions have schools or classes to learn about their religion. Literacy is considered important by religious adults because learning to read will ensure that their children become familiar with sacred texts.

Judaism

 Holiday of understanding

Research each of the five major religions to find out what each one teaches about peace and understanding. Create a holiday of understanding that uses elements from each of the five religions. What would you call your holiday? How would you celebrate it?

Christianity

33

A note to parents and teachers: ideas to promote tolerance and understanding

This book is the beginning of a process of discovering more about the world's religions and looking for commonalities among them. Here are some other things you can do with individual children or groups:

1. Research organizations and groups that are working to build peace and understanding between people of different religions in countries torn by religious conflict. Follow their work online. If you wish, write to them to let them know of your interest and ask what you can do to help.

2. Help children prepare an appropriate menu for a holy day feast for a faith other than their own.

3. Help children come up with their own definition of faith.

4. Invite a family of a different faith to one of your faith celebrations and join them in one of theirs.

5. Encourage children to pray for people of all faiths.

 Look for this symbol throughout this book for more activities to do with children. The fist bump celebrates working and being together.

Christianity

Glossary

baptism: a Christian ceremony in which a person (often a child) is welcomed into the community of the church

censor: a container for incense

communion: a Christian ceremony in which worshippers consume bread and wine, which are symbols of Christ's body and blood

enlightenment: in Buddhism, it is a special state of mind that is beyond suffering or desire

incense: material that releases fragrant smoke when burned

meditation: a process by which a person trains his or her mind to enter a different state of consciousness

miracle: a surprising event thought to be caused by divine intervention

offering: gifts (usually of money) made by worshippers of a faith

prophet: a person who has exceptional understanding of faith and spirituality

repentance: feeling sorry for having done something wrong

ritual: a form of ceremony

sects: groups within a religion who have different beliefs than other followers

worship: showing devotion to a divine being or beings

Countries represented in the photographs

Belize
Cuba
Malaysia
Mexico
New Zealand
Turkey
United Kingdom
United States
Vietnam

Index